Last Man Out

A personal account of the Gallipoli Evacuation

LOUISE PARK

wild dog

For those who in the face of adversity discover that there exists an opportunity to help others and do so.

L.P.

First published in 2023 by

PO Box 135
Fitzroy, Vic 3065
wdog.com.au

A catalogue record for this book is available from the National Library of Australia

ISBN: 9781742036427

Image colourisation: Quinn French

Printed and bound by Everbest Ltd.

10 9 8 7 6 5 4 3 2 1 23 24 25 26

We acknowledge the Traditional Custodians of Country throughout Australia and their connections to land, sea and community. We pay our respect to Elders past and present and extend that respect to all Aboriginal and Torres Strait Islander peoples today.
Aboriginal and Torres Strait Islander peoples should be aware that *Last Man Out* includes the names and images of people who have passed away.

FSC® is a non-profit international organisation established to promote the responsible management of the world's forests.

Contents

No doubt our mates on the transport cannot sleep at the moment because they all believe that the rear guard is doomed.

JOHN ALEXANDER PARK, DCM, MM

1915
Gallipoli

We cling to the steep hill, the sea at our backs, our enemies above us. A hill hollowed and honeycombed with trenches, tunnels, dugouts and observation posts. They carve their way across the Gallipoli peninsula, criss-crossing out and under the landscape. A peninsula squeezed between the Aegean Sea and the Dardanelles. Where our battles are fought. A mere 10 miles of steep, rocky land and rugged gullies that run towards the beach. A more hopeless ground for land battle could not be imagined.

During the past six months, the Allied forces and our enemy, the Turks, have engaged in the bloodiest of battles – Anzac Cove, Lone Pine, Sari Bar, the Nek and Hill 60, to name a few. They are a formidable foe, the Turks, and it is getting harder and harder to think of them as our enemy. We've helped each other bury the dead, traded cigarettes and bully beef, and shared a laugh, some notes, and a handshake. They are defending their country, their families and homes. Just like us. But we must harden our hearts and fight to win. Because, at the front, you survive or die.

Now, with deaths in the tens of thousands on both sides, this campaign has become a stalemate. We've dug in and refuse to be dislodged from this inhospitable cliff face. But we can make no headway in what has turned into a campaign of trench warfare.

These trenches, tunnels and dugouts are our fighting posts, our homes and our war strategy. For this campaign will be won by picks and shovels, by gaining another piece of ground, and by mines and explosives, and not by bayonets and rifles alone.

I am Sergeant John Alexander Park of the 4th Field Australian Engineers Company, Australian Imperial Force, and this is my Gallipoli.

September 12

Sickness, a constant companion

The swish, swish of summer dresses. Jennie and Kitty, their hands joined, smiles wide as they circle baby Gwen. Giggles gurgle up from deep within their bellies. Sweet innocent joy.

Ring-a-ring-o'-roses
A pocket full of posies
Atishoo, atishoo
We all fall down
The king has sent his daughter
To fetch a pail of water
Atishoo, atishoo
We all fall down
The robin on the steeple
Is singing to the people
Atishoo, atishoo...

The rattle of supply carts coming up the hill wakes me, and the escape sleep brings is gone. I roll from under my greatcoat, my back complaining as I straighten. I lift the oil sheet covering the entrance to our dugout and am met with an icy wind that smarts my eyes. A portent of winter. On it rides the smell of bodies we've been unable to bury. I glance back at my mates, still sleeping, and I hope their dreams are as soothing as mine. They need it. And then, beneath the crack, crack, crack of constant rifle fire, a lone bird sings, as if there is no war – a sound so rare it makes me fumble as I ready myself for another day – another day of advancing under enemy lines, where underground clashes continue, and battles play out above.

I grab our rations from the cart. Over-salted bully beef, tinned jam, biscuits hard enough to break teeth and not enough water to last the days that it must.

'Rankin,' I say, stepping back inside our hole in the cliff. 'Father Christmas has come.'

I get a moan for my efforts and give Owen a wink.

'Help me sit him up and get some water into him before we go.'

Rankin grimaces and water spills from his mouth.

'A slightly quieter night, must be on my way,' he

whispers. Owen and I lock eyes. Every Anzac knows that once you get the Gallipoli gallop, it can be deadlier than manning the trenches. And Rankin has it bad. I rest my hand gently on his arm.

'I like you better when you think you're whipping me at cards, chuckaboo. You need to be evacuated to hospital,' I say. But I know it will do no good. There is not a single one among us that wants to give in and leave, for any reason.

I hope these words don't come back to haunt me.

October 2

A prickly affair in No Man's Land

I am recording my recollection of the barbed wire incident before Owen's version becomes lore. A born storyteller is Owen, a gift we treasure in these conditions. But this particular story has grown more with each retelling, and I fear it is about to spread wings and fly. And given this is my journal, here it is in all its plain recounting.

'It's no good, get back!' I shout, ears ringing as bullets explode the dirt around me. Blood mingled with sweat trickles into my mouth. I am lying like a trussed-up turkey, in the middle of No Man's Land, the ground between the opposing front-line trenches. A place no man wants to be. I am wearing the wire entanglement Major Newcombe asked me to put up to stop the enemy coming closer. The sapper holding the end of the wire took a bullet and let go. Instantly, the wire coiled back on itself and shut me in. I am a neatly tied bundle with a tag saying, 'One prisoner going cheap.' The thought brings a chuckle.

More men in my party have been shot than not. I chose these men, brought them here under orders and their lives press down hard, causing an ache deeper than any bullet could achieve. Thank God Rankin is still in our dugout recovering.

'Get yourselves to safety,' I try to yell to the others. But it comes out as a gasp as the barbed wire makes a pincushion of me.

And then, as I inch my way towards our front line, I see him coming back for me.

'Come along then, mate,' Owen says, calm as ever. 'Head low.'

He helps me crawl back to our firing lines. At the top of the trench we find a loophole plate has come down. A sniper lets loose as we try to fix it back into position, and I am hit in a way I know will earn me a trip to Rest Gully Hospital. I need to move, but there is a rushing in my ears and my limbs are too heavy. Then Owen pulls me into the trench before the enemy can do more damage. Owen, my cobber, my dugout mate and one fearless soldier.

As I crash to the ground, I manage to mumble, 'No advertisements in our local magazine just yet, matey.'

Owen grins.

'To Let. Nice dugout with valley views. Owner leaving for field hospital.'

I try not to reward him with a laugh, and fail.

The thing about war, it underestimates us, the likes of Rankin, Owen and me. Our months of blistered, calloused hands. Of backs and necks pushing through the pain of dig, dig, digging in mines and tunnels. And all under the threat of enemy snipers. It has forged more than a friendship. We are a devoted brotherhood that has each others' backs. Our bond is stronger than life itself and the one thing war cannot take from us. But such strong bonds can be dangerous when dugout mates are there one minute and gone the next.

October 6
Rest Gully Hospital

The sea sparkles like a jewel on this cold crisp day. Anzac Cove is bathed in golden hues. For a split second, I wonder if this really is a war zone. Then the cries hit me like the sandbags that fall sometimes from the tops of our dugout. 'Can I have water!' 'Orderly, something for the pain, I cannot sleep.'

I am about to head back inside the tent when the soldier who has been on the stretcher next to me these last few days hobbles out on a makeshift crutch. I help him sit on an upturned crate and he mimes a smoking action. I pat down my breeches and hand him a cigarette and matches. And there we sit, looking out to sea in a companionable silence, sharing my last cigarette. Somehow, we manage to communicate that before all of this he was a farmer up in the Turkish hills and I was a driver. I show him the photo of my three little girls, and he shows me a photo of his family on his farm. Afterwards, I help him back onto

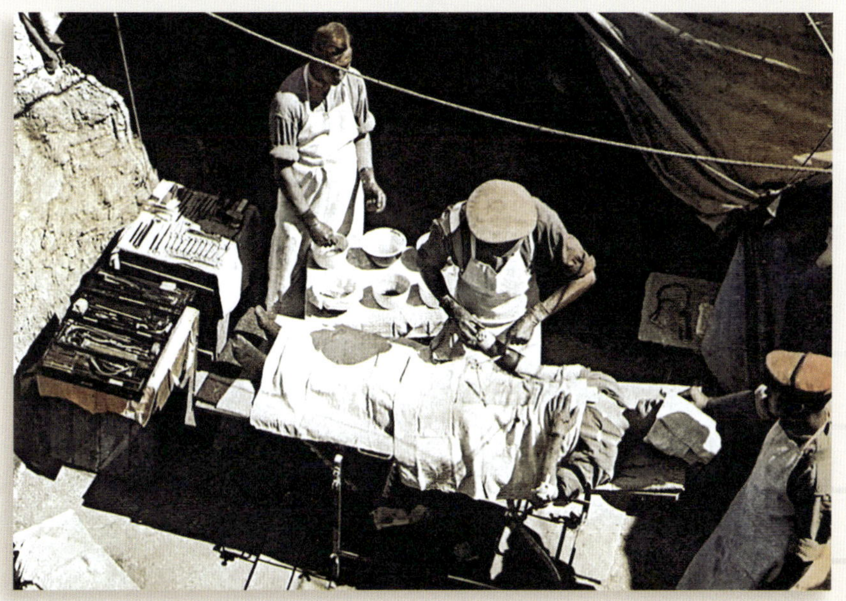

his bed and we shake hands.

Then it is time for me to leave. I know I am one of the lucky ones. I wasn't taken prisoner. Bullet removed, wounds dressed and an anti-tetanus shot onboard, I haven't needed to be transported to the hospital ships. I thank the medicos, who look dead on their feet, and as I pass my stretcher, I stop and say goodbye to my new friend.

'Good luck with it, take care.'

As I pick my way slowly and carefully up the ravine, I am consumed with so many thoughts I don't know how to sort them. In war we are equals – we bleed and suffer the same.

October 10
Moments of home

I emerge from a long night of back-breaking work in the tunnels and see that it's been raining while I've been under enemy lines. I groan at the thought of water sluicing its way through our dugout. My eyes adjust to the early morning light and I sense a shift. Instinctively, I know. Excitement and anticipation crackle in the air. I can feel it. It's mail day.

A digger calls, 'Get a wriggle on, Parky. You scored a package today.'

I burst into the dugout and laugh. Owen is all but bouncing on his bedding. Rankin is clutching a letter tightly. And on the wooden box we use for meals and card-playing sits a small package.

'Well, lads,' I say, eyeing the scene before me. 'I hereby request the Turkish troops withhold their ammunition and not waste it whilst the Australian Imperial Force stays in to read its mail.'

That brings a laugh as Owen hands me the package.

I nod to Rankin. 'Anything you'd like to share in there, first?'

Rankin folds the letter into his pocket, the one over his heart. He gives it a pat, then points to Owen, 'I've already read it aloud twice for this one. I'll tell you after, when he's off in the trenches.'

It's a given that when parcels and letters arrive, we share what we can. Home, for just a little while – that is what mail brings us. I let out a breath as I wrangle the box free from its packaging and open the lid. My eyes fall immediately on the tomato sauce and I toss it to Owen.

'That'll sort out the ration rot for a while,' I say, and a cheer goes up. I pass a container of tea to Rankin, who smiles broadly.

'Job well done, Mrs Park,' he says.

'Oh, thank you, my love,' I whisper as I lift out two pairs of woollen socks. A prized commodity. The colder weather and rain are taking their toll. Trench foot is already setting in and it's not yet winter.

'We'll play Two-Up for these when we are next together,' I tell my cobbers, placing the socks on the empty biscuit box.

Under the socks are drawings from Jennie and Kitty, a note from Ada and something slipped inside a Cadbury's Dairy Milk Chocolate bar wrapper. I collapse on my bedding and slip Ada's letter into my pocket for later. Jennie's picture shows a day trip to Coogee Beach. The level of detail is impressive for a seven-year-old. She's drawn herself standing outside the Coogee Palace Aquarium, looking very unimpressed. She must not have been allowed in. Underneath, she's written that they had a day by the seaside and the sun was shining. I close my eyes and images scurry across my brain. I see my girls frolicking and gambolling on the fine white sand that is so different from the coarse pebbly beach here. I cuddle the images so close I can almost believe my arms are around them.

Kitty's drawing is largely scribbles and swirls. Jennie has written underneath that they have both been missing prize nights with me of a Friday evening. That Mummy bought them a Cadbury block to share, just as though I was home. What's inside the Cadbury wrapper is my penny-bar share. Oh, my heart. One of them couldn't help themselves and has taken a bite off the end. I examine the teeth marks, and tears prick my eyes. I'm aware the boys are watching me closely as I smell the bar, eyes squeezed shut.

'I think it was Kitty,' I say. 'Or maybe it's Gwen. She'd have quite a few teeth now at 18 months. Either way, this bit is mine. You can split the rest between you.'

October 29
C2 mine under the enemy trenches

After months of digging and carrying we are finally under the enemy trenches, and we have orders to charge our C2 mine. It takes a company of infantry to pass the explosives and detonators along the low and narrow tunnels, lit by flickering candles in niches in the walls. The fatigue party detests handling the ammonal, but we engineers know the biggest danger is our enemy blowing up their tunnel first. If that happens, we are all done for.

'Here's the guncotton and more detonators,' Lieutenant Riddell says, handing them to me. Then he tells the fatigue party to clear out. We work quietly, packing explosives and fixing the guncotton and detonators in the heart of the charge. I steal a glance at Riddell. His hands are steady and sure. I trust his work as much as I know he trusts mine. We finish the job, the mine now ready for a blow.

Not long after this I am back in my dugout, when word passes quickly that the Turks have blown up their tunnel first. The blast causes the charge in our C2 mine to smoulder and release deadly gas. I grab Rankin and a rope and go.

Against a clear blue sky, I see the telltale gas clouds floating upwards. There is no time to think. I take a deep breath, hold it, grab the rope and drop down the 15-foot shaft into the tunnel. What greets me will visit me in nightmares for years to come. Lieutenants Bowra and Thom, Sapper Currington and several more are scattered about the tunnel, twisted into hideous, unnatural shapes. They are beyond human aid.

'Grab those with a pulse first,' I croak to Rankin. It's taken mere moments for my chest to feel as though a stack of our sandbags has been placed on it. I lift a sapper over my shoulder and begin to climb. My eyes, nose and skin burn like a lit flame. On our third descent, Rankin collapses, struggling to get air into his poisoned lungs. The sight causes my heart to miss a beat and I grab him next.

'That's one way to get out of work,' I joke, throwing him over my shoulder. Before I put him on the rope, I give his face a few slaps for good measure.

'Hang on for all you're worth or you'll have me to deal

with, you hear?' I watch to make sure he is hauled to safety before I head back down the tunnel.

When at last there is nothing more to be done, I tie the rope around myself. I know I am in trouble. My head is throbbing and I can feel myself slipping in and out of consciousness. The men haul me up, but near the top the rope slips, or is it me? I begin to fall. A big hand grabs me by the hair and another one wraps around my neck. The next thing I know I am being smacked hard about my back and face by field ambulance men, but I do not mind the rough handling.

'I'm all right, now,' I wheeze, 'see to the others.' But we all know my lungs are cactus.

'Thank God for the medicos,' I mutter as I watch them fighting to keep the survivors awake and breathing. I squeeze shut my eyes, but there is no unseeing what I have seen.

'Do you think you're able to help collect identity discs and paybooks from the dead, Park?' Colonel Moseley asks. I start at the sound of my name and wipe my face. It helps to know I'm not alone in my silent weeping. I pull Rankin to me and we hug, fierce and fast. Then, together, we attend to the dead.

November 5

A visit from the Royal Engineers and a bit of mischief-making

We are resting in the trenches, taking turns playing a game where we describe different scenes from our old lives. It is my turn and I'm glad. I know I am good at this game and the lads are looking low and in a bit of need. I go for the good ol' English fry-up.

'Baked beans warm in a pan on the stove. They bubble away, giving off a delicious tomatoey smell. Bacon sizzles and pops in the pan, crisping up in all the right places. The sausages, plump and juicy, spit as I gently turn them over. Tomatoes, ripe to the touch, are cut and ready to go under the griller...'

I see cobbers sniffing the air, as though my fry-up is about to materialise before their very eyes. Mouths hang open, lips are licked. Oh, the mundane ways in which we entertain ourselves before war crashes in on us again! No sooner have I begun to paint my glorious fry-up picture than Major Newcombe arrives from the Royal Engineers.

He asks me to assign him a batman. Now, no one wants to be a batman. Who'd be a personal servant to a commissioned officer when they can stay here visualising my fry-up? But needs must, and I detail Sapper Freddy Woods for the task. He is anything but happy about it.

Poor Woodsy, will he ever forgive me? To lighten the blow, I mischievously point out that opportunities for scrounging may present themselves. And sure enough, it doesn't take long for Woodsy to discover that the major has two bottles of aerated water. What a discovery! Better than gold, to be sure. Mischief again gets the better of me and I advise him to confiscate one to add to the fritters we make from pounded biscuits. Well, he didn't want the job anyway. But what a booting he copped!

There once was a young sapper called Freddy
As a servant, he was willing and ready
He took off with a bottle
And copped such a throttle
And that was the end of poor Freddy.

Mid-November

A visit from Lord Kitchener

41,218 men, 2,363 animals at Gallipoli

'What is that man doing with that tool handle and shell-case?' Lord Kitchener asks.

I look to General Birdwood and we exchange a brief smile.

'He's making a fritter by pounding a biscuit to flour, to which he will add some snow collected from the cemetery, a trickle of condensed milk and a little fat from a bully beef tin.'

I refrain from adding it'll also include a touch of Major Newcombe's appropriated aerated water.

'It's the only way to make the biscuits edible, and there's not much else to eat just now,' Birdwood adds.

'Marvellous,' Kitchener replies. He peers into the shell case and smiles. I risk a small wink at Birdy then turn to Lord Kitchener.

'Would you like to try some, sir?'

Birdy intervenes before Kitchener gets a chance to respond. 'Lord Kitchener would like to see the mines,' he tells me. 'Shall we go?'

I nod and lead the way. A tour of the mines, trenches and tunnels it is.

At mines C1 and C2, Kitchener goes down a short distance and asks, 'How far do they go?'

I tell him that we are under the enemy's trenches. He inspects the concealed firing line and then heads back to the trenches to speak with the men. I stand to the side and watch his eyes. I see the way he takes in the state of them and the conditions on this hill. Months of poor diet, dysentery, and a lack of clean water and warm clothing is taking its toll.

I see the way he is weighing his thoughts, and my gut twists. He thinks we are beaten.

Nothing is private in the dugouts, and I see my journal has had a visit from White. The cheek of it.

November 20
Kitchener's Apple Polisher
Johnston's Jolly
41,692 men at Gallipoli

Here's a drawing for you of your good mate Kitch. Now that you're in thick with our Secretary of State of War, put in a good word for me, will you? Fast pals, we hear.

Best,

Whitey

PS Freddy Woods still has half a bottle of aerated water, don't you know!

November 27

The Great Blizzard

41,208 men at Gallipoli

It's been the most miserable few days yet and it's brought home how very unprepared we are for the harsh Turkish winter.

Yesterday, torrential rain swept away encampments and dugouts. It flooded the ravines, taking hundreds of unsuspecting men with it. It filled the trenches with water that reached our necks. And today it snows, blanketing the hills in a carpet of pure white and bringing temperatures below freezing. The floods of yesterday are turning to ice. My greatcoat, soaking wet from the rain, is frozen hard and stiff enough to stand up on its own.

Wind howls down the gullies and icicles hang from the trenches and tents. Mud clings in clods to the men's boots as they bury the dead in cemeteries scattered among the valleys. The men slip and slide; bones are broken. More than half of us is suffering from frostbite. Hundreds have lost their lives to it and it feels as though we are losing more men out of the firing line than in it. I wonder how our enemy is faring. Not a lot better than us, I suspect. The one bonus of these dreadful conditions is that it's brought a pause from fire on both sides.

Despite our state, those of us that are still standing with moving limbs remain determined. There is not a single one among us that would walk away. Still, there is a whisper on the wind, one that no man wants to hear or believe. Has Kitchener really recommended we evacuate Gallipoli? Surely not, although I fear this blizzard might just be the nail in the coffin.

November 30
A guest artist on fashions of the season
40,668 men at Gallipoli

Thanks for the laughs, Scotty of the 4th Battery Field Artillery. We sure needed them.

December 11
Evacuation plans
36,011 men at Gallipoli

The shock of evacuation orders rips through the Anzac troops like a seismic tremor, affecting each man deeply. Disappointment at abandoning the campaign so strong that many men and several officers, including Birdwood, would rather instead we blow our mines and make a last gallant dash at the enemy. Misery weighs heavy at the thought of leaving our hard-won trenches, the mines we've taken months and months to dig – our cobbers lying in their graves in cemeteries, No Man's Land, the valleys and hillsides. I know not a soul that wants to give up.

Incredibly, as men grapple with this news, we learn that an evacuation plan is already in operation, and that after all this sacrifice and suffering we are going to attempt to sneak away, unseen – a plan that many believe will end in heavy casualties and disaster. But there it is, and I struggle to bend my frazzled mind to it. In no

time information is passing along the lines faster than ammunition. We are told that troops will evacuate by stealth in stages, and that a rear guard of honour is to be selected for the last group to withdraw.

And so, the rivalry begins. Who will be chosen to stay on until the end? Who will hold fast to the last to allow tens of thousands to slip away silently from Gallipoli? Only the fittest, the most gallant and capable will be chosen. The pick of the whole force, we are told. And the message is clear: the rear guard of honour will be killed or captured. The rear party, the most daring men of all, doomed.

It is a suicide mission, but a mission that the men desperately want to be a part of. Anzacs are imploring their officers to include them in the last troops to leave, to retain honour and dignity. And I, with my damaged lungs, am determined to be one of them.

December 13
Shrapnel Gully Cemetery
26,193 men and 500 animals left

'Did you make it into the rear guard, then?' Owen asks, holding the cross steady.

We are in Shrapnel Gully Cemetery. For days there has been a constant stream of men in our cemeteries. They come alone, in small groups, to say their goodbyes. To tidy the graves, erect crosses and offer earnest apologies at planning to scurry away, secretly, like mice, leaving them behind.

'Did you?' I ask Owen in return, for I know a man of his calibre will have begged for the privilege.

'Don't know yet,' he replies, 'but I'd better.'

And the weight of things left unsaid makes it hard for me to breathe.

We carry on together, and alone, lost in our own private farewells. As we leave to go our separate ways, we hug.

'See you in the Shepherds,' he says, shaking my hand suddenly.

‘Meet me in the Wassah and don’t stand me up, you hear,’ I reply.

Owen’s steady gaze pierces my facade.

‘Just make sure you stay standing, cobber, you hear?’

And I know that he knows. He always could read me like a book. During the past week, even the slightly sick and wounded have been evacuated and many of the hospitals and field ambulances withdrawn, their tents left standing to give the appearance they are occupied as usual. It is rather spooky seeing the tents with only a few stretcher bearers left in them. Evacuation is well and truly underway. But will our ploys be enough to fool the enemy into thinking our entire force is still here?

9am, December 18

Courtney's post — cold and cloudy with a high chance of enemy attack

20,277 men left

'That's the last of them,' Riddell says, dumping a pile of bully beef tins at my feet.

'The boys at Lone Pine are using water. What if the candles burn out before the string is released?'

I shield my face from the watery winter sun.

'Not much we can do. We've not enough water left,' I say.

Riddell and I are constructing devices to make rifles self-fire. I run the next piece of string through a candle and attach it to a bully beef tin filled with rocks and dirt. Later, when there are just a few of us left we'll attach the strings to rifle triggers to hold them back. Then we'll light the candles. When they burn through the strings, the triggers will release, firing the rifles. Scurry's invention, being used by some other troops, works a similar way.

A top tin is attached to the trigger and filled with water. Water drips slowly from a hole in the bottom of the tin and fills the tin below it. When the bottom tin is full enough, the weight pulls the trigger and the rifle fires. We Anzacs are an ingenious lot when push comes to shove.

Riddell raises an eyebrow and says, 'When the last of us withdraw, this is what will save our backs.'

Our eyes meet, and the unspoken words lie heavy between us. If Jacko Turk attacks anytime between now and then, he has a wonderful opportunity.

11pm, December 18

Of muffled boots and more goodbyes

10,000 men left

For the last two days, our depleted troops have practised walking with their feet wrapped in pieces of blanket to muffle the sound. Now that the time has come for the men to withdraw, an overwhelming urge to go with them hits me like a dose of Gallipoli gallop.

'Godley will have handed over to the Rear Guard Commander by now, as planned,' I say to Riddell.

We watch the last of them go, quietly padding down ravines towards the beach. Riddell claps a hand on my shoulder. He turns me away from the gullies that lead to the transport waiting to take our mates to the ship, and to safety.

'You'll stay to the last, to help me fire the mines if they attack?' Riddell's eyes do not leave mine as he waits for my reply.

'There was never any doubt in my mind,' I say, surprised at how steady my voice sounds. 'But let's hope we hold this pretence for the next four hours and it does not come to that.'

Back in the trench, I try to still my trembling hand as I shave and wash in a condensed milk tin of water. Today we've managed our usual level of gunfire, kept small cooking fires going even though there is nothing left to cook, and done all else we could to keep up the charade of normality. Groups of men were even given the job of loitering or having a cigarette, as though on a break. Not quite as effective as the cricket match on Shell Green yesterday, but it all adds to the illusion. Was that really only one day ago?

5:45pm, December 19

Hold fast to the end, lads

6,000 men left

The moon is shining, casting shadows in the bottom of the trenches. A scene so peaceful it is at odds with my rolling stomach. It's been a day of heavy shelling, with a mere 6,000 of us left to do the work of more than 40,000 men, and not just on the front lines. We've also been busy burying ammunition in the latrines, destroying our pickaxes, tins and cooking pots, and pouring caustic soda on the tarpaulins – a job my lungs weren't up to. Bombs, rifles, food, clothing, boots, shoes and anything else not needed by the rear guard are gone. Soon, all that will be left to show we were ever here will be our trenches, dugouts and mines, and our brave, loyal cobbers sleeping in their graves.

The A party has just withdrawn and the front lines begin to feel ominously deserted. As the garrison makes its way down to the beach, orders are given that we

must hold the lines to the last. We need to hang on at all costs and, if necessary, blow the mines to stop the enemy advancing. We are told the parties leaving this night are under strict orders not to return to the line to help us. Not under any circumstances. We all resolve to die rather than be captured. God help us. My mind turns to Rankin and Owen. Rankin should be on his way to Egypt by now. As for Owen, I do not know, but I tell myself he has already evacuated. I cling desperately to this belief.

11 pm, December 19

C party, a bloomin' picnic

2,000 men left – the rear guard of honour

Riddell and I are making trip-wires, to which we will attach grenades. Everyone is on rotation. If they aren't in the trenches firing as many guns as they can, they are busy setting up booby traps. Trip-wires, like the ones we are making, are attached to dugout doors, furniture and tents. It is my duty, I know, but it gnaws at me. You see, I respect them, the Turks. This campaign, it's been a battle of opposing sides that seem to know and understand each other, as people. They dig deep to defend their homes and families, just like us. We are the same, yet different. We could easily be friends, yet we are foes. How could we ever despise them, when we are them? I wish I could meet them in another time and under more mutually desirable circumstances.

Riddell breaks into my thoughts, as though he can read my mind.

'You know,' he says. 'Minus the ones on the beach aiding the retreat, there's really only about 1,500 of us up here. Fifteen hundred holding 10 miles of trenches. There's no way we'd survive an attack right now.'

I lay my trip-wire on the pile and consider whether there is enough trip-wire to string across the trenches once the self-firing rifles have been set up.

'C party were hand-picked. They are the steadiest. The finest shooters. The most disciplined.' I give Riddell a wink. 'We are a handful of men doing our best to sound like an army, but we are a first-rate handful.'

A ditty we sing about hardening your hearts starts in my brain and sets my teeth on edge.

Boots, belt, rifle and pack
All you'll need till you come back
All you'll doff when you lie down to sleep
All they'll take off when they bury you deep
Boots, belt, rifle and pack.

2:15am, December 20
Approximately 100 men in the trenches

'Only the self-firing rifles are left,' Riddell tells me. 'The whole of the northern half of the Anzac trenches are empty.'

I feel sweat on my forehead, despite the freezing temperature. All the mines are laid and ready for us to blow when the time comes. My back feels broken from the task.

My voice is barely a whisper as I ask, 'Any indication they suspect what we are up to?'

Riddell shakes his head and I feel my shoulders drop. 'They are none the wiser,' he says, 'and apparently they're still erecting barbed wire entanglements to keep us back.'

I haven't allowed myself to think even for a second that we might succeed. I joined the rear guard knowing what our fate would be. I finish erecting our wire entanglement. I can't remember when I slept last – days ago, maybe. I raise my eyes to his and laugh. Riddell has a smile on his face as wide as can be and he gives me the thumbs up.

'Well, isn't that the best piece of news,' I croak. 'Any water left in your bottle? I haven't had a drop since yesterday.'

Riddell shrugs. 'You and me both,' he says. 'You and me both.'

Then the troop number drops to 60, and the men spread out.

2:40am, December 20

24 men in the trenches

A thick mist smears itself across the moon and the firing gets heavy. It's war as usual, except on our side only 24 men hold the trenches. Where shortly before the men were covering every third and fourth bay, they now have to run back and forth between six and more to fire the rifles and keep up the illusion of an army of men.

'It's just like an interstate cricket match,' says one of the men. 'Eleven on either side and two umpires, one on the telephone and the other on the exploders.'

That brings a laugh, all right, as we all run ragged. Our cricket teams are spread from Wire Gully to Lone Pine and from Courtney's Post to Russell's Top, and every state in the Commonwealth is represented in these last 24 men. Both flanks are now blocked with wire entanglements and, if we are lucky to leave without being killed, we will all go out via the gully. The question is, will the enemy wake up?

No doubt our mates on the transport cannot sleep at this moment, waiting to see what is going to happen. They believe the rear guard is doomed.

Some time after 3am, December 20
22 men leave the trenches

Riddell is on the phone calling me.

'The party on the right is coming out,' he states. 'Leave your exploders and stop them. They need to wait until the party comes out from the left.'

These are the very last of C party, and when they arrive I tell them to sit a while. The Turks fire and a shell lands somewhere towards Shrapnel Gully. I think to myself that our self-firing rifles are all that will respond from now on. My stomach churns.

The party from the left arrives and joins the waiting men. It is time for them to head to the beach. But it's hard to get them moving. None of us has slept for three days and it is now almost dawn. These men are loaded with packs and rifles and the adrenalin that has kept them going is all but gone. These men, the selected rear party who never expected to survive, are collapsing from sheer exhaustion, some of them asleep on their feet.

'It's been an honour,' I tell them, 'to have seen this thing to the end with you. But if you don't up and go, I will boot you along!'

And as they stumble away helping each other down the track, their feet wrapped in scraps of blanket, they say, 'Goodnight, engineers, are you not coming?'

My throat is so tight I cannot rustle up a reply. I wave them off and, as I do, I know that the extraordinary valour and devoted brotherhood of this motely lot – the rear guard of honour – will stay with me forever.

Around 3:30am, December 20
And then there were two

The trench is now empty except for two engineers, Lieutenant Riddell and me. It is getting a bit lonesome now. I close the wire in the sap, pull the entanglement across the road and stand by the exploders. Looking up to the trench, I pretend I don't see Riddell looking at me. I smile to myself and wonder what he is thinking. I am wondering whether they'll leave a boat for us. I can tell he is thinking the answer is no. And I expect he is right.

'Good God,' I say to myself, 'shadows moving about on the ridge. Do they know? Are they coming for us?'

My hand tightens on the exploders but my heart stays steady. I am ready, come what may. I look back at Riddell and think what a great cobber to have at a time like this, one of the finest, a real man. If I am to die, then there is no better man to be with than him.

Riddell is on the phone talking to someone. When the conversation is finished, he indicates that we have to destroy everything and make haste to the beach.

Our last group will be there by now. We are to leave without blowing the mines. I detach the electric cable from the exploders and kick dirt over the ends of the instantaneous fuse. Then I take up my rifle and use the butt to smash the exploders.

'Don't make so much noise,' Riddell says, drawing a finger across his throat.

For the minute I had forgotten there were just us two. Anyhow, Jacko Turk would think it was the cooks breaking up a box to light a fire to boil the dixies.

Around 3:45am, December 20

The last man out

I sling the telephone on my back and we gather our gear and start down the track. Near the cutting going through from the ravine to Shrapnel Gully and the beach, I step off the track.

Riddell says, 'This way.' But I need to dump the gear that must be destroyed.

'Go on ahead, I'll catch up to you.'

I can see him looking around, and he shivers. It is so very eerie – the deserted trenches, the empty dugouts with candles burning, as though cobbers are still in there. A sight that ten days ago I could not have imagined.

I head to the area where we engineers had been sinking for water and drop the gear in. Then I stop one last time at the cemetery and say my final farewells.

'Sleep soundly and peacefully,' I whisper.

Please God, don't let them know we are going from them forever.

I make my way down the steep dark track but cannot see Riddell.

It's just me, alone in the gully, the last man out. I look back up the hill, my home for these past months.

'Farewell brave and unrelenting Turks, you've been grand. Take care.'

Eventually I catch up to Riddell, who has just sprained an ankle. I help him along the last stretch and as we move, arms tightly around each other, I say, 'Shall we take bets on whether a boat is waiting?'

4am, December 20

The beach

As we hit the sand and take in the scene, we both begin to shake. The relief at the sight of a boat waiting to take us to the transport is immense and our bone-weary legs can all but hold us upright. I lean forward, resting my hands on my thighs and take deep breaths. Riddell covers his face with his hands.

'We did it,' he whispers through his fingers.

I place a hand on his shoulder and rub my eyes with the other.

'More than 40,000 men, horses, supplies – the works. And only one mine exploded. We did it. With no sleep, nor food or water.'

I stare at the unexpected, unbelievable site of the boat as Riddell reports to the remaining few officers on the beach. Coupled with sheer exhaustion, it is too much and I cannot take it in.

Dawn, December 20

Farewell to Gallipoli

It is now daylight, and the officers in the ship's saloon are having something to eat. Riddell brings me out some bread and meat and I sit down between two diggers. I turn to offer them my food, to go 50–50 with them, and who should it be but Owen.

'Well, aren't you a sight for sore eyes,' I tell him, clutching him to me. 'Thank God.' I wipe my face with filthy hands.

I ask him if he has any water in his bottle.

'Only a drop,' Owen replies, grinning. 'And it's all yours, mate.'

COPY 25 Sept 33

THURLBY HALL
Lincoln.

Dear Mr. Park.

Many thanks for your letter the details of which bring back to me so vividly the happenings of that wonderful night of the Evacuation, which was so splendidly carried out by every single man ashore, & every one of whom will I am sure look back with real & justifiable pride to the part played by him & all his comrades. I wish I could help you in the matter about which you write - the more so as C.C. Riddell is a cousin of mine (my name too), but I fear I am unable to do so. I have to say this as you will probably realise I have had at least a dozen letters all on just the same lines as yours, claiming to have been the last man to leave the shore that night or later early morning, to all I have only been able to say as I do to you - I was up & down the coast all night in H.M.S. "Chatham" - the night was dark & embarkation took place simaltaneously at several points along the coast. Those on our extreme left when we joined "Suvla" claim they were the last - you also do so! What I can say is that you occupied a most important position & from what you tell me you evidently carried out what was entrusted to you capitally. I only regret you had no orders to blow C.1. & C.2. also! But as you know I was in command of & responsible for both Anzac & Suvla then & naturally could not go into all details at both places. At all events I am very glad you did however come through everything as you did & it is a pleasure to see how fit you are now 18 years after & so young still! All good wishes to you -

Your old comrade.

W.R. Birdwood.

Much has been written regarding the last days on ANZAC — as to the anxiety of the staff, the misery of the men at leaving behind those hard-won trenches, and the cemeteries of brave cobbers. But the valour and devoted brotherhood of the selected last few hundred — the rear guard of honour — linger longest in my memory.

John Alexander Park, DCM, MM

Author's note

Last Man Out is a personal account of the withdrawal from Gallipoli based chiefly on my grandfather's letters, published articles and notes detailing his experiences and movements up to those last moments on Gallipoli. His articles have been quoted in numerous war books on the subject and are accepted as a most reliable eye-witness testimony. But this book isn't only about him. It is about a group of people who chose to put themselves on the line for the sake of tens of thousands of others. It is about digging deep and finding out who we are and who we don't even know we could be. It is about ordinary men doing extraordinary things. And it is about loyalty, having each other's backs no matter what, and valuing something greater than yourself.

Although taken directly from my grandfather's accounts, a book like this cannot be written without a mountain of research behind it. The Australian Imperial Force unit war diaries; the diaries, notebooks and records of war correspondent and official historian Charles Bean;

battalion war diaries of the final stage of the evacuation; the correspondence, letters and notes from Lieutenant General William Birdwood and Lord Kitchener; and many fascinating hours in the company of the good folk at the Australian War Memorial's research centre and reading room have helped shape my retelling of grandfather's account.

My grandfather died long before I was born, but I grew up listening to my father's anecdotes about him. From those stories, I recall that my grandfather simply felt he was just doing his job, like everyone else, friend or foe, and that war was the greatest equaliser because in war we all bleed the same. Based on his letters and my father's anecdotes, I've gleaned much about his personality but, like any narrative nonfiction, I've had to imagine some conversations and incidents to weave this into a compelling story. All the soldiers in this book are real and no offence is intended towards them or any living relative of the soldiers that I have included in the service of telling this account.

Charles Rankin was indeed a great friend of my grandfather. He was his dugout mate and cobber, as was Sapper Woods. Just like my grandfather, Charles Rankin

was also awarded the Distinguished Conduct Medal for his coolness and courage during rescue operations at C2 tunnel opposite Johnston's Jolly, ANZAC, and for his efforts to rescue men disabled by gas fumes from ammonal explosion. In the medal citation for my grandfather's DCM, it mentions the above and that he descended a shaft 16 feet deep by a rope ladder several times in his attempts to rescue disabled men although he was badly gassed in his first descent.

The DCM awarded to my grandfather was also for his evacuation work. Specifically, for his excellent work and untiring devotion to duty during the withdrawal from ANZAC and the preceding week in preparing and laying the mines for explosion after withdrawal of the troops if necessary. The medal citation outlines that he waited until after the departure of the last troops from the trenches in order to close gaps in barricades and wire entanglements, and that the work was of a highly technical nature and was performed in a very efficient manner.

The C2 explosion, the wire entanglement incident and spell in Rest Gully Hospital, assigning Sapper Freddy

Woods as Major Newcombe's batman and asking him to confiscate an aerated bottle of water, the visit from Lord Kitchener and the subsequent interaction with Kitchener and Birdwood, and the account of those last days and moments of the evacuation are exactly as my grandfather recorded them. He and Lieutenant Riddell were together until the very end and separated only for my grandfather to dump the gear that had to be destroyed and say his goodbyes. When they joined up again Riddell had indeed sprained his ankle and was helped to the beach by my grandfather.

Francis Edgar Owen was an Aboriginal man. He was transferred to my grandfather's company, the 4th Field Company Engineers in August 1915 and rather than wait for his company to be deployed he stowed away on a transport ship and landed at Anzac Cove on 28th August. For his efforts Owen was charged with conduct 'to the prejudice of good order and disciple' and sentenced to 14 days field punishment no. 2 (confined to barracks) before being allowed to join his company, as a sapper on 25 September. Owen

remained with his unit on Gallipoli until they were evacuated. I know that my grandfather knew him well and was with him until the final evacuation. They were the same age and I could well imagine these two men having the friendship portrayed in this book. However, I am not sure he was the one who helped during the wire entanglement incident. I do not know who that was. Nor did the conversation in Shrapnel Gully cemetery take place.

At the time Owen enlisted, Aboriginal people were not recognised as Australian citizens. It is estimated that between 400 to 800 Aboriginal men fought in WWI.

I could not pin down exactly when Charles Rankin and Francis Owen left Gallipoli, only that it was before my grandfather. Likewise, I do not know whether Rankin picked up the Gallipoli gallop but given the number of soldiers struck down with it, it is highly likely.

The drop in the number of men in those last days and hours at Gallipoli was recorded in the evacuation plans, but they do vary slightly according to various sources. I have made every effort to be correct in these numbers and times, cross-checking as many sources as possible.

Evacuation of Gallipoli
Special Order of the Day
General Headquarters
December 21, 1915

The Commander-in-Chief desires to express to all ranks in the Dardanelles Army his unreserved appreciation of the way in which the recent operations, ending in the evacuation of the 'ANZAC' and 'SUVLA' positions, have been carried to an issue successful beyond his hopes. The arrangements made for withdrawal, and for keeping the enemy in ignorance of the operation which was taking place, could not have been improved. The General Officer commanding Dardanelles Army, and the general Officers commanding the Australian and New Zealand and 9th Army Corps, may pride themselves on an achievement without parallel in the annals of war. The Army and Corps Staffs, Divisional and subordinate Commanders and their staffs, and then Naval and Military Beach staffs, proved themselves more than equal to the most difficult task which could have been thrown upon them. Regimental officers, non-commissioned officers and men carried out, without a hitch, the most trying operation which soldiers can be called upon to undertake — a withdrawal in the face of the enemy — in a manner reflecting the highest credit on the discipline and soldierly qualities of the troops.

A Lynden Bell, Major-General,
Chief of the General Staff
Mediterranean Expeditionary Force.

I will always remember those men — probably the pick of the whole Force, and they looked it, despite their ragged appearance; some with full beards, while the lean cheeks of the others were covered with several days' stubble.

Second Lieutenant George McIlroy,
24th (Victoria) Battalion,
6th Brigade, 2nd Division, AIF

Glossary

ammonal: an explosive

ANZAC: Australian and New Zealand Army Corps

batman: a soldier or airman assigned to a commissioned officer as a personal servant

bayonet: a stabbing or slashing instrument of steel, made to be attached to or at the muzzle of a rifle

bully beef: tinned meat, especially corned beef

cobber: a mate; friend

DCM: Distinguished Conduct Medal

ditty: a poem intended to be sung

dixie: a large metal pot in which stew, tea, etc. is made

doff: to remove, as in remove clothing

dugout: a rough shelter or dwelling formed by an excavation in the ground or in the face of a bank, especially when part of military earthworks

dysentery: an infectious disease marked by inflammation and ulceration of the lower part of the bowels, with diarrhoea that becomes mucous and haemorrhagic

front: the front line in a battle, the line of contact of two opposing forces

Gallipoli: The Gallipoli peninsula is located in the southern part of East Thrace, the European part of Turkey, with the Aegean Sea to the west and the Dardanelles Strait to the east

Gallipoli gallop: dysentery

garrison: a body of troops stationed in a fortified place

guncotton: or nitrocellulose (also known as trinitrocellulose and cellulose nitrate) a mild explosive

identity disc: worn about the neck, it was stamped or engraved with the soldier's details

latrine: toilet, especially in a camp

loophole plate: plate built into a parapet to allow a soldier to see out of a trench without exposing his head to enemy fire

MM: Military Medal

niche: a recess in a wall to hold candles

paybook: a document carried in the top right tunic pocket which was proof of identification both as a battlefield casualty and when receiving pay

sapper: soldier who performs combat engineering duties — usually digging trenches and was often a member of a military unit of engineers

saloon: a large cabin for the common use of passengers on a passenger vessel

[the] Shepherds: an area where soldiers gathered for a drink and chat

trench: a long, narrow excavation in the ground, the earth from which is thrown up in front to serve as a shelter from the enemy's fire

two-up: a gambling game in which two coins are spun in the air and bets are laid on whether they will fall heads or tails

Wassah: an area in Cairo known for its nightlife. Also referred to as Wazza, Wozzer, Wassir, Wasser, Wassar, Wazzir. Several riots by ANZAC troops in this area became known as the Battle of Wassah

Front cover image: H.C. (Henry Charles) Marshall, State Library of New South Wales; **Back cover image:** From The Pictorial Panorama of the Great War embracing Egypt, Gallipoli, Palestine, France, Belgium, Germany and the navy – from an exhibition of war photographs in natural colour. Colart's Studio (Melbourne, Vic.) detail, State Library of New South Wales | Map depicting the Anzac position at Gallipoli. State Library of Victoria; **endpapers**, Collected correspondence, private collection of the author; **pp.1**, Map depicting the Anzac position at Gallipoli. State Library of Victoria; **pp.4**, John Alexander Park, DCM, MM, private collection of the author; **pp.8**, Landing stores at X Beach, Cape Helles, near Seddulbahir. Gallipoli Peninsula, Turkey. c May 1915, detail, Charles Snodgrass Ryan, State Library of New South Wales; **pp.11**, Graves on the front, detail, State Library of New South Wales; **pp.13**, Australian soldiers taking cover in trench (possibly during shelling). State Library of Victoria; **pp.14**, First aid and evacuation of injured soldiers, detail, State Library of New South Wales; **pp.17**, Medical corp in action at Gallipoli, Turkey. A doctor and nurse working on a patient in a hole. State Library of Victoria; **pp.20**, Soldiers drinking tea from tin mugs, and eating bread and jam (1914 –18) State Library of Victoria; **pp.21**, Cadbury chocolate packaging, source, Cadbury, image manipulation, Donna Rawlins; **pp.25**, Scene in the trenches, detail, State Library of New South Wales; **pp.29**, Lord Kitchener and his generals, 14/11/1915, detail, G.Downes photographs of Gallipoli during World War 1, 1915. Mitchell Library, State Library of New South Wales; **pp.30**, "Kitch", C. Leyshon-White, drawn with an iodine brush, *The Anzac Book*, National Library of Australia; **pp.33**, ANZAC Fashions, Winter, A.H. Scott, *The Anzac Book*, National Library of Australia; **pp.35**, Two Australian soldiers digging trenches (1915) State Library of Victoria; **pp.38**, Kensington to Cairo and from Cairo to Gallipoli. 1914 – 1915 album of photographs (attributed to) H.C. Marshall, detail, State Library of New South Wales; **pp.41**, Drip gun; **pp.45**, Kensington to Cairo and from Cairo to Gallipoli. 1914 – 1915 album of photographs (attributed to) H.C. Marshall, detail, State Library of New South Wales; **pp.48**, detail, Gallipoli and Egypt. Vol.02, Mitchell Library, State Library of New South Wales **pp.51**, detail, Gallipoli and Egypt. Vol.02, Mitchell Library, State Library of New South Wales; **pp.52-53**, Adobe Stock; **pp.59**, H.C. (Henry Charles) Marshall, State Library of New South Wales; **pp.60-61**, Kensington to Cairo and from Cairo to Gallipoli. 1914 – 1915 album of photographs (attributed to) H.C. Marshall, detail, State Library of New South Wales; **pp.63**, Photomontage, Quinn French; **pp. 64**, Letter from W.R. Birdwood to J.A. Park, private collection of the author; **pp.66**, Kensington to Cairo and from Cairo to Gallipoli. 1914 – 1915 album of photographs (attributed to) H.C. Marshall, detail, State Library of New South Wales; **pp.69**, Kensington to Cairo and from Cairo to Gallipoli. 1914 – 1915 album of photographs (attributed to) H.C. Marshall, detail, State Library of New South Wales; **pp.70**, ANZAC – Making jam tin bombs, detail, G.Downes photographs of Gallipoli during World War 1, 1915. Mitchell Library, State Library of New South Wales; **pp.73**, Frank Edgar Owen, *The Queenslander Pictorial*, supplement to *The Queenslander*, 19 June 1915, State Library of Queensland; **pp.74**, Lord Kitchener's farewell salute at ANZAC, 14/11/1915, detail, G.Downes photographs of Gallipoli during World War 1, 1915. Mitchell Library, State Library of New South Wales; **pp.76**, G. S. McIlroy, 'Silent Stunts: Turks Outwitted' *Reveille*, 1/12/1932; **pp.78**, From The Pictorial Panorama of the Great War embracing Egypt, Gallipoli, Palestine, France, Belgium, Germany and the navy – from an exhibition of war photographs in natural colour. Colart's Studio (Melbourne, Vic.) detail, State Library of New South Wales.

Still, the process of evacuation continued steadily during the five nights ([illegible] to [illegible] December), and although it was not possible to [illegible] all the vehicles and stores, [illegible] guns and [illegible] of all [illegible] were shipped to Mudros (see Appendix I "Table showing daily evacuations from Anzac").

(ii) The measures taken to conceal our intention from the enemy aimed at the preservation of normal conditions in every respect; while, by ordering the complete cessation of all hostile action for periods of from [illegible] to [illegible] hours, it was hoped to accustom the enemy to periods of silence. It is probable that the three days "silent [illegible]" which we carried out during the last week of [illegible] [illegible]. On that occasion, the enemy displayed marked uneasiness and eventually counterattacked our line in several places, suffering many casualties. A summary of the measures taken is given in Appendix II.

6. Our intelligence reports for some days prior to the withdrawal indicate that the enemy was quite ignorant of our intention. He probably imagined that our designs were aggressive, for he continued digging, and adding wire to, his defences all along his front up to the very end.

7. Particular care was taken to bury stores, that could not be removed or destroyed, beyond the reach of [illegible] were placed a few feet below any covering of [illegible] ground.